HP & ME

HP & ME

My Little Corner of the World

BY

HP AMES

HP & Me

Copyright © 2019 by HP Ames. All rights reserved.

No part of this publication may be reproduced, stored in a retrieval system or transmitted in any way by any means, electronic, mechanical, photocopy, recording or otherwise without the prior permission of the author except as provided by USA copyright law.

The opinions expressed by the author are not necessarily those of URLink Print and Media.

1603 Capitol Ave., Suite 310 Cheyenne, Wyoming USA 82001
1-888-980-6523 | admin@urlinkpublishing.com

URLink Print and Media is committed to excellence in the publishing industry.

Book design copyright © 2019 by URLink Print and Media. All rights reserved.

Published in the United States of America

ISBN 978-1-64367-603-6 (Paperback)
ISBN 978-1-64367-605-0 (Hardback)
ISBN 978-1-64367-604-3 (Digital)

01.07.19

My Little Corner of the World

BY H P AMES

Dedicated to the life and memory of Brian Wesley Ames

April 2, 1957
December 21, 2017

INTRODUCTION

MY LITTLE CORNER OF THE WORLD by Harold Peter Ames: Author, Actor and Thinker for the Seniors of the Brave New World, and Spokesperson for Each of us in Thirty Adventures.

Introduction by J.J. Hurtak, Ph.D., Ph.D.*

Good news! You did not wait 60 years for nothing! I'm proud to announce a new book by a dear friend entitled, *My Little Corner of the World*. H.P. Ames has given us Thirty Adventures of Wit, Wisdom and Philosophy. H.P. Ames is a 92 year old senior, a former Banker, Realtor, and Financial Planner and Actor who retired in San Diego and has seen it all. But more importantly, H.P. has seen *the Light of new life* at his ripe age, and realizing happiness is a state of mind, he reveals his secret wisdom for all occasions. As a former actor at the Great Coronado Play House in San Diego, he learned to use this guiding light through personal trials and tribulations to find the joy within. H.P. has learned the secrets of good thinking and laughter which he shares with us in his adventures that enlighten our body, mind and spirit.

The great thinkers revealed their secrets to the common people of their time in complex art and science. There can be, however, a more basic key to human nature and life itself in the written and spoken stories each of us can experience. We can create within ourselves an inner Temple of Understanding in our "Little Corner" for the adventures of Life. We can use the "golden years" of our life to think and see "golden Light" in the greater proportions of joy and balance in wisdom and wit. Yes, we can use the hours of our life daily to focus on the Light of wisdom and positive reflections to improve our lives, our health, our happiness with others. The great thinkers and poet-scholars were inspired by realizing the Light of Divine inspiration with insights through which they described Life in special ways. This is also the work of H.P. Ames as we listen to his words of wisdom.

In H.P.'s small, but compact book of adventures, we can connect to his stories of life. . As we hear the mellifluous voice of the H.P., let us close our eyes and concentrate on our body as a beautiful garment of Light surrounded by little gems of light.

Our memories of life can be soothed in the journey of Life. Actor and super sleuth H.P. Ames, however, shows us how our "Little Corner" of the universe can be filled with love and understanding. He unravels, perhaps, the greatest mystery of all time, a life code that seems to underlie all our actions of life by the decision we make to visualize the Light, concentrate on the Light, and use our golden years to find meaning in the way we share our positive thinking with others. With wit and insight, we begin to feel the vibrations of good energy between the u every level of life. Let us always go with the Light and listen to the wisdom and wit of H.P.

Listen to each chapter of this audio book which introduces that which is sacred, simple, pure, natural, open, humble, peaceful, other worldly, truthful, strong, light, delicate, clear and transparent, sweet like honey, strong and vulnerable. It can create within us a healing power, guiding us into a gentle space, relaxing, receiving, offering, making us feel graceful, holy, happy, anything but ordinary. . In general, we are too busy to receive the gift each person brings to us. Joy calls us now, to receive the best of everyone, and we must take the time to realize each experience. We can never listen too much.

The themes presented in this book, *My Little Corner of the Word*, remind us to receive our true wit and happiness flowing through, around, and in between each chapter of the book as we adventure into re-discovering our powerful heart presence. We have energies to heal the divisions of our lives within and without. When we understand this, we realize the current circumstances of our lives are close enough to perfect.

H.P. would like us to listen and honor our hearts, to nourish ourselves deeply and unfold our true self into the world with our renewed lives giving the best of our story of life to our fellow humanity so that we can take the higher path.

And now, beloved listener, be inspired as you hear the important message that goes with each chapter of our "Little Corner" of life on Mother Earth.

*J.J. Hurtak is a Futurist with the Academy for Future Science, a United Nations NGO (non-government organization) working worldwide in education and song among the Developing Nations in southern Africa and South America.

PREFACE

Welcome to H P and Me, and My little corner of the World, featuring the wit wisdom and philosophy of H P Ames 92 years on the planet Earth. For close to a century HP has participated in the evolution of modern society and has observed the many pitfalls which have plagued humanity in it's wake.

"My Little Corner of the World" attempts to address some of these issues and provide witty philosophical insights into how to live a better life. Join "HP and Me" for a little "Chicken Soup for the Mind, the Heart, and Soul.

The following transcripts are from the radio/podcast of "HP and Me: My Little Corner of the World," which commenced airing in 2018.

CONTENTS

THREE QUESTIONS 1
MARCUS AURELIUS 4
FOREST FOR THE TREES 7
WE TAKE SO MUCH FOR GRANTED 10
SECOND CHANCE 13
IF I KNEW THEN 16
HESITATION 18
GUARDIAN ANGEL 20
LETTING GO 22
YOU ALWAYS HURT THE ONE YOU LOVE 24
IT'S THE LITTLE THINGS THAT COUNT 26
A GIFT FROM GOD 28
INTIMIDATION 32
DIALOGUE: 34
DON'T BURN YOUR BRIDGES BEHIND YOU 37
BAD LUCK CAN BREAK YOU OR MAKE YOU 40

- YOU HAVE TO BE HUNGRY TO WIN 42
- IT'S NOT OVER UNTIL IT'S OVER 45
- MIRACLES DO HAPPEN 47
- YOU HAVE TO BREAK THINGS TO FIX THINGS 50
- YOU WILL BE SURPRISED AS TO WHAT YOU WILL SEE AND HEAR IF YOU LISTEN 52
- BE CAREFUL: STRAIGHT TREES OFTEN HAVE CROOKED ROOTS 54
- A BED TIME STORY FOR THE MIND AND SOUL 56
- BE HAPPY IN YOUR WORK 58
- PAY FORWARD 60
- LOVING; THE SECOND TIME AROUND 64
- EVERYONE HAS SOMETHING IN THEIR PAST THAT THEY WOULD LIKE TO FORGET 67
- BEING AT THE RIGHT PLACE AT THE RIGHT TIME 69
- YOU CAN'T ALWAYS HAVE OR GET WHAT YOU WANT - BUT YOU CAN TRY 72
- BEFORE YOU WONDER, AM I DOING THINGS RIGHT ASK AM I DOING THE RIGHT THINGS 75

THREE QUESTIONS

Before we can answer the questions of life–"Where do we come from?" "Why are we here?" "Where do we go?" --we must carefully ask ourselves three essential questions that H.P. Ames poses for us to think about in this series. The blueprint of life is within our careful thoughts and reflections.

Welcome to My Little Corner of the World:

Many years ago someone once said, "The world is yours for the taking" but there are three questions that you should ask yourself first. Question number one: do I want it? Question number two: what is it going to cost me? And Question number three: is it worth it? The rest is academic – think about it.

Well it all boils down to this: As to question number one, do I want it? Well, what do we really want? Is it good health, happiness, a happy marriage, raising a family, wealth, helping others, loving one another, by that I mean do unto others as you would have others do unto you etc.

Now, all of these are worthy wants, now as to Question number two; What is it going to cost me? By that I mean what do I have to give up or compromise or do to achieve the above goals? It's academic, just try and do what you can to the best of your ability. Do whatever is right. Listen to your conscience, let your conscience be your guide. Remember my friends you will never, never, know when you are right.

And, as to Question number three: Is it worth it? And the answer is "YES", yes to all of the above except monetary wealth. Because all the money in the world will not buy any of the above. There is an old saying, "Never use money to judge wealth Ergo never judge wealth by money. All you have to do is look around you and you will see how wealthy you really are. Remember, there is another saying, "You cannot see the forest for the trees." Likewise, "You don't know what you got till its gone. Think about it my friends. This is H P signing off and wishing you that the bird of plenty give you peace, tranquility, happiness and good health, and until we meet again, love you to the moon and back, God Bless.

MARCUS AURELIUS

Marcus Aurelius, the great Roman Writer and Philosopher, once wrote about doing more with our life within the short margins of our material existence. H.P. teaches us that we can do more with the power of our life in inspiring people no matter what our situation is. It is the art of the impossible made possible!

Welcome to my Little Corner of the World:

Marcus Aurelius once said in his meditations something to the effect, "If a person or persons can do or accomplish the so called impossible, so can you too accomplish the impossible. Think about it! So many of us take the attitude or posture that unfortunately I cannot do it. I'm not that gifted etc. They give up too easily because it's the simplest way out. Just remember that you and you alone control your destiny. All you have to do is try to accomplish the so called impossible. Just try and you may surprise yourself. Nothing in a sense is impossible. A few years back I saw a movie called, " One Flew Over the Cuckoo's Nest" staring Jack Nicholson.

The scene takes place in a mental institution. One afternoon Jack Nicholson and his so called inmates are in a recreational area. They seem/appear to be extremely depressed. They don't care, they want to give up. So Jack Nicholson decides to do something about it. In the center of the area is a washbasin sink bolted into the concrete floor. He then says to his inmates, "I will bet you that I can rip this sink right out of the floor." The inmates then look at him and say (pardon the pun if you will) "You're crazy as all get out!" They then take the bet. Nicholson makes a first attempt to try and rip the sink from the concrete floor and fails. Then he tries a second, third, fourth attempt and fails. His inmates now look at him and laugh and say "We told you so." However, Nicholson looks at them and says, "At least I tried... at least I tried." Think about that one.

Don't be afraid of failure. Someone once said, "Failure leads to success." Sir Winston Churchill, former Prime Minister of England said (WW II), "We will Never, Never, Never give up." So, I say to you my friends, "Never give up. If at first you don't succeed then try, try again." I would like t thank the author of that quote. Remember, you can do it... Think about it! I mean, really think about it.

This is H P signing off and wishing you that the bird of plenty give you peace, tranquility, happiness, and good health. Until we meet again, I love you to the moon and back, God Bless.

FOREST FOR THE TREES

The secret and mastery of our life is in the lifestyle of how we put the four-letter word "Love" into unconditional action without limitation. Love is the powerhouse of our existence and our genetic identity no matter what our age. The outreach to do more with our life comes through our daily use of the greater benefits of Love.

Welcome to My Little Corner of the World:

There is a saying, "You cannot see the forest for the trees." How true. Do we really take the time to appreciate what we really have? We take things for granted. Remember, nothing is forever, not even diamonds. Live each day as if it were your last. Who knows what tomorrow will bring, or if tomorrow will ever come. Take time to appreciate your loved ones, your family, your friends, your neighbors etc.

Remember, "People who need people are the luckiest people in the world." It's nice to be able to share your life and wonderful moments with others. There is nothing worse than to come home to an empty house and have no one to share your priceless moments of the day. There's a tremendous void, believe me. As I mentioned in one of my previous radio shows, "You don't know what you've got 'till its gone." Really think about that one!

The world is so full of hate, greed, bigotry and being jealous etc. My friends, these are the biggest things we have to fear, because they can destroy you, they can kill you, they will kill you. What a waste of energy. Why not use this energy, this powerful tool for a four letter word called LOVE.

Why not work together as brothers and sisters to promote good will and love. We should try and work hard to promote peace, harmony and love and to try and get along with one another. Remember, in unity there is strength. Now, you may say that this is a crazy dream. Well dream big, because dreams do come true. Barbara Walters once said, "Be careful what you wish for, because it may come true. Let this dream come true. Remember, the mind and the will is a very powerful tool. Think about it, I mean really think about it!

This is HP signing off and wishing you that the bird of plenty give you peace, tranquility, happiness and good health, and until we meet again I love you to the moon and back, God Bless.

WE TAKE SO MUCH FOR GRANTED

We travel on the highway of life as pilgrims on Mother Earth. There are good ways we can use the power of our mind to steer us ahead so that we can daily overcome the challenges we face and carry on with the Joy of Life. H.P. has given us pause to get down to the roots of consciousness.

WELCOME TO MY LITTLE CORNER OF THE WORLD:

Alan, this is a so called follow up regarding my last radio show. I mentioned then that we take so much for granted. We cannot see the forest for the trees. We continue to make stupid silly mistakes. Again and again not knowing why. Remember, your mind is a very powerful tool. You can psych yourself to do almost anything. However, you have to believe in yourself first.

At the end of the day ask yourself; did I learn anything from my mistakes? And if you can honestly and truthfully say, "Yes" you did, then all is not for naught. Because you survived, and now you are a lot smarter than the other person because he has yet to be tested to see if he now can or will survive. You are now the Guru of the mountain because you made it.

Now, as you travel the highway of life and you see and encounter other pitfalls, you now have enough sense to side step them or to get out of the rain and onwards and forward to bigger and better things in life. You made it! Remember, we are all human beings and we all make mistakes. It's no crime to fall flat on your face. The real crime is rolling over and dying. You pick yourself up, brush yourself off and come out fighting. Everyday we have the so called unexpected happen. The things you take for granted all of a sudden go down the drain. Nothing is forever, not even diamonds.

Your going to have days where good things happen and where bad things happen. That's life my friends, but it all depends on how you handle both. The good and the bad. Because that will determine your character. It's very easy to handle the good things. But it takes strength, determination, and character to handle the bad things.

When the going gets tough, the tough get going! You can do it if you believe in yourself. Just do it! Think about it. This is H P signing off and wishing you that the bird of plenty give you peace, tranquility, happiness and good health. Until we meet again, I love you to the moon and back! and God Bless.

SECOND CHANCE

Life gives us a 'Second Chance' to find and use a peaceful and harmonious way of life in service to the Divine and to humanity. By using the Golden Rule we find the 'Peace that passes all human understanding," that is, a genuine Man-God partnership beyond the crazy material things people accumulate. The power of truth shows us that we are part of an Infinite Way.

WELCOME TO MY LITTLE CORNER OF THE WORLD:

You know, so many of us have said from time to time, "If only I had a second chance, if only I had a second chance." Well, a second chance is possible. In order for this to happen to you, you have to be honest and truthful to yourself and to the Man above. Especially to the Man above! If the sincerity is there, then maybe you will have your second chance. Now, should you be given that so called second chance you will be tested as to your truthfulness etc. as to how you will handle this precious gift of having a second chance.

Will you squander this opportunity or really fulfill your promise? The question is now, how and what will I now do that's going to be or make a difference. Will I squander the opportunity on crazy material things such as living a ridiculous silly monetary life and only thinking of myself? Or think of others and share with others and give to society and the world contributions that will make a better world? To practice the Golden Rule; do unto others as you would have others do unto you. And yes, to be nice to yourself also.

You will see in doing these things the satisfaction, mental and physical that you will be granted with. You will now be living a very peaceful and fulfilling life. It is a wonderful feeling to be able to share with your brothers and sisters this peace, harmony and tranquility. In doing these things all of us will be living a better and tranquil world.

Think about it….really think about it!

This is H P signing off and wishing you that the bird of plenty give you peace, tranquility, happiness and good health. Until we meet again, I love you to the moon and back! God Bless!

IF I KNEW THEN

Years of experience can give us better perspectives of Life and how to achieve inner greatness. Joy found in the midst of great difficulty is joy found forever. The Divine spark is always available for us to use. H.P. cues us from his ninety-two years of experience.

WELCOME TO MY LITTLE CORNER OF THE WORLD:

"If I knew then what I know now," how many times have we said that? A Lot! Then was the time that we knew it all. No one person could tell us anything, especially our parents. They were older, more mature and had lived through many great experiences and survived. They had the wisdom of real experiences and real life. They probably forgot more than we will ever know. As a result, again, we would not listen because we thought that we knew it all. How wrong we were. We knew nothing and through the years we learned the hard way.

We made many numerous mistakes, and at times we had no one to bail us out. We really learned life the hard way. We said gee, as we are growing older our parents are getting a lot smarter. No! We were beginning to mature and realizing how stupid we were. Some of us were more fortunate to have had the opportunity to mature and grow up at an earlier stage of life and to have listened to our parents and elders and benefit from their worldly experiences, which enabled all of us to really further our wisdom and education and to be able to contribute to society and the world and become scholars of contribution to the making of a better world.

There is a saying, "Be a good listener, because that's how you learn. Never be afraid to ask questions, because that's how you learn. Do things to the best of your ability. Just try and you will succeed. You my friends will do and can do the impossible and achieve greatness, if you try. This is H P signing ff and wishing you that the bird of plenty give you peace, tranquility, happiness and good health. Until we meet again, love you to the moon and back, God bless.

HESITATION

Life offers many opportunities and we should not feel inhibited in exploring new ways of life. We should go beyond 'hesitation' and not be shy to be open to the moments of pure life that feed us no matter how easy or difficult, light or challenging, long or short, our lives maybe.

WELCOME TO MY LITTLE CORNER OF THE WORLD:

Did you ever get ready to do something and then hesitate? In doing so you ask yourself should I or should I not do it. Then based on gut feeling you do it. You now ask yourself was that the right decision? You did something based on instinct and instinct only and wonder now if you were right. As I mentioned in a previous radio show, you will never, never know when you are right. Don't be afraid to take a chance. Do whatever you feel is right! It may not be the right way, but it will be "your way."

Sometimes the so-called wrong way may be the right way for you. Do whatever you feel is right. You and only you know yourself and your capabilities. In doing the so-called "right way" it just may be the wrong way for you. Do whatever you feel is right to get the job done and the final results that you were striving for.

Who are we to say what is the right way or what is the wrong way. It's the successful results that you achieve that will be the right way. In doing so you may encounter some regrets and some mistakes, but you will also encounter success!

As Frank Sinatra in his song, "My Way," "You did it your way" congratulations! So I say to you my friends, don't be afraid to listen to that gut feeling. Think about it!

This is H P signing off and wishing you that the bird of plenty give you peace, tranquility, happiness and good health. Until we meet again, I Love you to the moon and back! God Bless!

GUARDIAN ANGEL

The word 'Angel' means someone who is willing to help another no matter what the cost. Modern scientists may call them 'ultra-terrestrials,' beings from distant or higher worlds. In reality, however, the meaning of angel is in remembering the greater Love and Joy that nourished us. Love does not come by accident or coincidence. In sharing the promise of a greater Life with someone, we truly unfold our true self into life as Human-Angels!

WELCOME TO MY LITTLE CORNER OF THE WORLD:

Do you or I have a Guardian Angel? I would like to believe that we do. Angels come in different forms. Did you ever receive a helping hand from someone you knew or did not know? Receive help or whatever from unknown sources, and wondered how you lucked out or how did this happen? The so-called unexpected and unexplainable happenings. Well, the good Lord acts in strange ways, but he sure gets the job done.

Could it be that some of us are the angels and couriers and messengers for the man up above, and as a result carrying out the good deeds where needed in helping someone? You at the time may be a Guardian Angel. Doing unto others as you would have others do unto you: The Golden Rule.

So, again I ask you, is it possible that you or I may be an angel at a specific time and place and helping someone in need at the time. Are you or I an angel? This my friend is something we will never know. Remember that angels do come in different forms.

Let's be good to one another, and you will see how blessed we really are. Let's practice in loving our brothers and sisters and learning the true meaning of love. Remember, as in the movie, LOVE STORY, "Love means never having to say you're sorry." Think about it!

This is H P signing off and wishing you that the bird of plenty give you peace, tranquility, happiness and good health. Until we meet again, I Love you to the moon and back, God Bless!

LETTING GO

WELCOME TO MY LITTLE CORNER OF THE WORLD:

How many of us have experienced moments of great tragedy and sadness and disappointment in life? Yes, all of us have at one time or another have neglected to capture the moment. Again, we take things for granted. Those were the days my friend, I thought they would never end. That's what we would like to think. But alas, everything does come to an end. That my friend is the cycle of life. Now we ask ourselves the question of how do we handle the situation. Are we capable and strong enough to do this. This is where character sets in. It's not easy! But here's where the tough get going.

The tragedy of a death, of someone you, all of us, have loved dearly comes to an end. The shock is devastating. There is a tremendous void. You are now in limbo looking for a place to land and there is nothing in sight. You want to hold on, but now you have to let go, but you fight desperately to hold on, but now you have to let go. And finally after a long period of time you do let go.

There is a saying, " With time, you will come to terms" ergo, you will come to terms with time. We may let go, but we will never forget! We will always cherish those precious moments that, at the time, we did not capture.

You will always have moments of tragedies, sadness and disappointments. You have to be strong, and with the help of the man up above you say to yourself, " Tomorrow will be the beginning of a new dawn, a new day and a new life. And life goes on with or without you. So, now you say to yourself, "Onward and forward to a new life." Never dwell on the past, because it can prevent your future.

I know my friends, because I have been there, and I survived, thanks to the man upstairs. My friends, you too can do it! Just think about it!

This is H P signing off and wishing you that the bird of plenty give you peace tranquility, happiness and good health. Until we meet again, I love you to the moon and back, and God Bless!

YOU ALWAYS HURT THE ONE YOU LOVE

We should be more sensitive to the ones around us. Joy and compassion slows down from the energy of the daily world to life's beauty and wisdom which we should beam through our eyes and broadcast through our words. We do not hurt the ones we love if we are truly God-centered in Light.

WELCOME TO MY LITTLE CORNER OF THE WORLD:

How many times have we said or done things that later we have regretted is saying or doing? Too many times! We have a tendency of doing these things without thinking first. There's a saying, "THIMK before you louse it up." You may have noticed that I said THIMK. Spelled T H I <u>M</u> K instead of think spelled THI<u>N</u>K. Because that's what we do, we don't THIMK before we louse it up. Words are very precious and powerful. And as a result, we should be careful before we speak. Because in not thinking before hand you may and can hurt the one you love, "The one you shouldn't hurt at all." We should be considerate of one another. People have feelings and we should respect this. Again, be nice to one another. It's the little things that count! You know, we don't have to do things in a big way to capture someone's attention. It's what comes from the heart that really counts. The real thing: love and consideration and being nice to one another.

It's so easy to criticize, but so difficult t give praise to someone that has earned it! We are jealous of doing so. This is where hatred sets in. As I mentioned in a previous radio show, be careful, "Jealousy can destroy you, Jealousy can kill you, Jealousy will kill you! Be nice, be good, be careful in what you say, and remember The Mills Brothers song, "You always hurt the one you love, the one you shouldn't hurt at all." Think about that one! This is H P signing off and wishing you that the bird of happiness give you peace, tranquility, happiness and good health. Until we meet again, I love you to the moon and back, God Bless!

IT'S THE LITTLE THINGS THAT COUNT

Do not be fooled by the illusion of "big things" or false posture. The little things in life add up and train us to nourish ourselves deeply and unfold our true self into the world, molecule by molecule. We go onward and forward in life no matter what by being the avant-garde for the little sparks of life we can cultivate each day.

WELCOME TO MY LITTLE CORNER OF THE WORLD:

So many times, we go out of our way to try and impress someone or somebody. In doing so we want to do things in a very big way, because we feel this will impress them if we do something "BIG," "Very BIG." Well, "BIG" is not necessarily better. It is a false power or vibration that we are sending out. We are not being honest with ourselves or others with this type of false posture. We are trying to be somebody that we're not! We are human beings and we are not stupid! A lot of us will sense this falseness. You in a sense are not fooling anybody. There is a saying, "You can fool some of the people some of the time, but you can't fool all of the people all of the time."

We should try and be ourselves and not someone we are not! Do things because you want to do them. Do things because it comes from the heart. Do things because you are sincere and not false in doing so. Do things because you really mean it. It does not have to be "BIG."

Remember, it's the small things that count. Be honest, truthful, sincere and mean it. We the people will now sense this honesty and now we will be impressed! In doing this you will now have achieved what you originally set out to do. You have impressed that someone or somebody. Now, onward and forward to achieving your original goal. Remember my friends, it's the little things that count! Think about it, I mean really think about it! This is H P signing off and wishing you that the bird of plenty give you peace, tranquility, happiness and good health. Until we meet again, I love you to the moon and back! God Bless!

A GIFT FROM GOD

Life can really be a roller coaster until we find the 'ocean of peace' in this moment. That is when we give our self to the inner retreat, our place of being where we nourish ourselves by the 'Peace' that God brings. We overcome depression and limitation by learning how to expand our consciousness through new heights, breaths, depths, and lengths that come with the visualization of limitless light and space.

WELCOME TO MY LITTLE CORNER OF THE WORLD:

In life there will be many failures. Some of us will take failure for granted and do nothing about it because it is the simple way out. In taking the simple way out we will hit rock bottom and stay there. Others will take "NO" for an answer and try to do something about it. It will take strength, discipline, determination and guts to pick yourself up from the gutter and try and start a new life. To do something about it. It's not going to be easy, you're going to have to have faith and believe that nothing is impossible.

You will have to believe in yourself and in God. And in doing so, you will be able to do it. You have to remember that life will never be that simple. Life is a roller coaster with many ups and downs. Here is where you tell yourself, "Mind over matter." Because the mind is a very powerful weapon. You can almost do anything once you make up your mind. Remember also that life can be beautiful. It's what you do with what you've got and have that will make the difference and count in the end. The question is now, do you have the determination and guts to do it? Yes, some of us become very depressed at times because we have lost someone very dear to us or we have suffered another type of tragedy in life, or for whatever reason, and we now feel that life is not worth living. Life is a precious gift from "GOD" that should not be squandered or taken for granted. A lot of us fight and try to extend this precious gift, and there are others that squander this gift by committing suicide and thinking that this is the simple easy way to bring things to closure.

How wrong can they be! In doing so it may be over for them, but for the rest of us that are left behind it becomes very painful. It hurts, and we hope with time, the pain or hurt will become easier to cope with. But not so! Maybe for some of us, but not for everyone. You know, before you try and take the easy way out, "THIMK" (spelled T H I M K not T H I N K) before you louse it up for "you" and everyone else. Life can be beautiful. You have people, friends, and family out there that love you and want to, and will help you.

As I mentioned in an earlier radio show, "People who need people are the luckiest people in the world." Let us destroy this negative virus of depression, hate, jealousy and inject us with a serum of love, compassion and being totally positive on life. In being positive, considerate, compassionate etc. you may not know it, but you in being alive could and will be making your contribution in this world. Don't destroy this precious God given gift of life by self-destruction. You have been given a "priceless gift."

Again, I ask you, do you have the "Guts" to do whatever is right? To live life! I think you do! I know you do! Do It! Think about it, I mean really think about it!

This is H P signing off and wishing you that the bird of plenty give you peace, tranquility, happiness and good health. Until we meet again I love you to the moon and back! God Bless!

INTIMIDATION

As we grow older and wiser we realize that intimidation and bellicose behavior never works When we have high values and ethics in our little corner of the world we are available to take the higher path and be touched by our Divine essence, the living beauty that unfolds slowly, gently from the heart that carries luminescence sparks that are resilient. We continue to manifest the Light no matter what the physical situations of life.

WELCOME TO MY LITTLE CORNER OFTHHE WORLD:

When we were young some of us were constantly intimidated by others. As we grew older, the intimidation continued. There are people out there that constantly thrive on intimidating others. When we were young we called it bullying. Now we call it intimidation. The person doing the bullying was usually with 6 to 8 of his so-called buddies, never alone.

As time went on and we grew older, it continued, but now we call it intimidation. The rules are a little different. Now the attack is executed by trying to degrade, slander, abuse, ridicule etc. This makes the person doing this have a false feeling of power and strength and so-called integrity. They think that you will not fight back. How wrong can they be! You do fight back strong and hard.

When people try to intimidate you it's because they are jealous and envious of you. You are way up there, and they are down below looking at you up above and being envious of you and what you have accomplished and stand for: your high values and integrity. They are extremely jealous of you and they want to take you down to their embarrassly low level. You say "NO," and as a result become victorious and they loose and sulk in their own hatred etc.

Stand tall! You have now achieved victory! You have now won! They have lost! You are now the winner! Think about it! Really think about it! This is HP signing off and wishing you that the bird of plenty give you peace, tranquility, happiness and good health. Until we meet again, I love you to the moon and back! God Bless!

DIALOGUE:

We do not sit or stand in isolation in a busy world. We must speak up on questions that involve positive solutions for neighbors and for the human race regardless of culture. Our openness, creativity, the strong feelings of our heart can convey real meaning for those who look to us for answers. In self-realization we live in our true ground of being a NEW BEING.

WELCOME TO MY LITTLE CORNER OF THE WORLD:

All of us at one time or another have exchanged words with others in a derogatory way. Later we regretted in what we said. We at times did not know how to communicate our feelings of remorse. We kept silent and thought that the problem would go away, and all would be well and normal, as though nothing ever happened. However, the problem did not go away. It was still there, as big as ever.

In keeping silent, our minds begin to wander and we start to interject crazy meanings of why we are not hearing from the other person. As the silence continues the so-called problem becomes more problematic. It grows as in the play, "Uncle Tom's Cabin," like Topsy! We are now making a mess of the situation.

Communication, dialogue is the solution to most problems as a rule. Not everything can be resolved by dialogue but, it sure comes close! In communicating, we open all channels of doubt and now the mind is not wandering and jumping to erratic conclusions. Now we know the facts, and we now know how to handle the situation in a proper manner. As a result, bringing the problem to a realistic closure. Again, not always, but a majority of the time. Remember my friends, silence is not always golden. Dialogue has a tendency to clear the air and get things back to a so-called normal status. Again, as a rule. Think about it! Really think about it!

Tis is H P signing off and wishing you that the bird of plenty give you peace, tranquility, good health and happiness. Until we meet again, I love you to the moon and back! God Bless!

DON'T BURN YOUR BRIDGES BEHIND YOU

In the cross roads of decision making and making new directions we must not cut ourselves off from friends and family who have supported our path of development. We must not burn our bridges with those who have given us meaningful activity in the journey of life. There are no limits to love's potentiality.

WELCOME TO MY LITTLE CORNER OF THE WORLD:

You know, as we climb the ladder of success, sometimes we forget to remember and thank and stay in touch with some of the people who went out of their way to help us in achieving our goals. We forge ahead as though we never needed anyone to help or assist us n achieving our success. We seem to think and believe that we did it by ourselves. How wrong can we be!

In now forging ahead, things seem to fall in place like magic. We are now on a roll. Nothing seems to go wrong, or that they will go wrong. We can't loose! Nothing can stop us! Well, wrong again. It's like the ocean: the tide goes in and the tide goes out. All of a sudden, things begin to turn against us. In many cases we did not prepare for the unforeseen! Not thinking that there can be a rainy day. We did not prepare nor did we stay in touch with the people that did help us before.

We seemed to have thought that it would not be necessary to prepare for the unforeseen, or not necessary to stay in touch with the people that were there before and helped us. Wrong again! We burned our bridges behind us. A big mistake! You got to remember, in life we will always need people ie. Friends, relatives, family etc.

Again, as I mentioned in a previous radio show, "People who need people are the luckiest people in the world." Don't try and be proud and think that you can do it by yourself. Maybe you can, and some of us can do it by ourselves. But in many cases you will need that someone to help you! Don't burn your bridges behind you! Think about it! Really think about it!

This is H P signing off and wishing you that the bird of plenty give you peace, tranquility, good health and happiness. Until we meet again, I love you to the moon and back. God Bless!

BAD LUCK CAN BREAK YOU OR MAKE YOU

As we mature we realize that misfortunes and so-called "Bad Luck" can break one's spirit, or serve as a springboard for new understanding of Life. Remember, there are no problems, only solutions for those who can grasp the greater light. This is the time that what the ancient prophets and mystics called Hesed, or heartfulness, can give us permission to explore new directions of life's call. Something greater is with us, in us. We must listen to the rhythms that pervade all life and bring us the simple joys of the garden of life we cultivate within.

WELCOME TO MY LITTLE CORNER OF THE WORLD:

How many of us have heard the quote, "Bad luck can break you or make you." How true! In life we will face many adversities. Sometimes one after another and we will ask ourselves when will it ever end? No matter what we do it seems to backfire on us and it goes on and on and it appears that it will never stop. And it won't if we allow it to get the best of us. That's when it will and can break us. We can do something about it. Again, it's going to take strength, discipline, determination and guts! Here's where you pick yourself off the floor and come out fighting! In taking this posture you can and will change the coarse of adversity. Now, with this attitude you are now heading on a positive coarse of having good things happening to you. Here's where you took bad luck and turned things around to a positive note. You surprised yourself! You did not think that you had it in you, to take tremendous adversity and turn things around. You now look at yourself with pride, dignity, confidence etc. You took bad luck and turned it into good luck. Whereby making a strong person out of you and not the weak person that you were before. Remember, bad luck can break you or make you. Have it make you! Again, remember you can do it! Think about it. Really think about it!

This is H P signing off and wishing you that the bird of plenty give you peace, tranquility, good health and happiness. Until we meet again, I love you to the moon and back! God Bless!

YOU HAVE TO BE HUNGRY TO WIN

In a world of hard knocks and disappointments we need to come back up from the floor of bad investments in time and energy. The fine tuning of our soul can be a shining mirror of how our soul can be reawakened and strengthened from the higher values of art, music and new science. Here the creating of a personal "sound space for soul growth", or a little room for positive thinking, can initiate new levels of golden moments which can be real food for a hurting heart.

WELCOME TO MY LITTLE CORNER OF THE WORLD:

How many of us have heard or are familiar with the saying, "You have to be hungry to win." Well, that was a quote by Jack Dempsey one of the greatest heavyweight boxing champions of the world. He was tough, rough, but always a gentleman. He came from the school of hard knocks. He had to fight for everything in life. Nothing was easy. It took blood, sweat, determination and guts to fight his way to becoming one of the greatest heavyweights in boxing history. He said, "You have to be hungry to win." You have to want something with all your heart to achieve the goal of being great. No matter what that goal may be. You have to have heart! With this credo he achieved greatness. He fought many a battle in the ring. One of his greatest fights, "Dempsey VS Tunney," was historical and was called the "Long Count Fight." Jack Dempsey and Gene Tunny fought round after round, head to toe. It was a thriller! Finally, Dempsey knocked Tunney down and went to a neutral corner. The referee started the count. However, Jack was in the wrong corner. The referee then told Dempsey to go to the right neutral corner and then started the count again.

With the so-called long count, Tunney was able to get up and fight. Tunney won the fight later by a decision. Now, if not for the long count, Dempsey would have won the fight by a knockout. Wow! What an ending! Yes, there were many great heavyweights, and Jack Dempsey was one of them. He truly was Great! Remember my friends, you too can be great, but you have to have heart and be hungry! Be hungry and achieve greatness. You can do it. Yes, you can. Hey, here's to a healthy appetite! Think about it! Really think about it!

This is H P signing off and wishing you that the bird of plenty give you peace, tranquility, good health and happiness. Until we meet again, I love you too the moon and back! God Bless!

IT'S NOT OVER UNTIL IT'S OVER

In the world of business, global politics, or baseball, the final fiat accompli is NOT necessarily the final fiat accompli –when there's comeback with extra life. Remember life is part of a living continuum which can provide understanding of our lives connected with the ongoing breath of evolution that does not stop with Mother Earth. Life is a calling to the inner river of higher consciousness. H.P. Ames is right on target!

WELCOME TO MY LITTLE CORNER OF THE WORLD:

How many of us in our so-called lifespan have taken the posture or attitude when involved in certain situations, taken the stance that it's "Over" when it was not over. We have a tendency to give up all too easily. We don't have the "Balls" (if I may use that word) or the courage to hang in there when it appears to be over. Whether we are at a sports event or involved in a business transaction or everyday situations in life, we don't have the "Balls" to see the situation through to its ending and see how it actually ends. When we do, Boy are we surprised as to how wrong we were in our jumping to a wrong conclusion or ending.

It did not end that way we thought it would. We should not give in or give up before it's over.

Yogi Bera, former catcher for the New York Yankees, one of baseballs great athletes once said, and I quote, " It's not over until it's over." You know, people laughed at that quote or saying, stating what a stupid remark made by Bera. How stupid was it? Not stupid at all. It was brilliant! They should have asked themselves, how stupid was their remark! Remember, "It's not over until it's over." Thank you Yogi Bera for your wisdom. You were one smart "cookie," if I may use that word. Our friend Yogi Bera is no longer with us on this planet. However, he will be well remembered as a great person and a great athlete. And again, "It's not over until t's over." Think about it! I mean really think about it!

This is H P signing off and wishing you that the bird of plenty giver you peace, tranquility, good health and happiness. Until we meet again, I love you to the moon and back. God Bless!

MIRACLES DO HAPPEN

New findings in psychology as pioneered by leading scientists at Stanford Research Institute-have shown that the elevation of human consciousness is connected with minor miracles, e.g., mind-over-matter, bending forks and spoons, and remote viewing of things in Russia simply by the power of the mind. We must be open to a new era of synthesis between scientific and spiritual truths.

WELCOME TO MY LITTLE CORNER OF THE WORLD:

How many of us really do believe in miracles? Well, miracles do happen. Has this ever happened to you while you're driving your car and all of a sudden there is a car collision where many cars are involved and there is no way that you can avoid being part or being involved in the collision. You try and step on your brakes. Your car begins to sway in every direction and you begin to pray and hope that you can avoid being part of the so-called mess. Your car is swaying in every direction, and you say to yourself, "This is It!"

Somehow your car comes to a crazy stop and you have avoided being seriously injured. Or, you become ill and all the prescribed medications and everything else that you try and do seems to not help your situation at the time. Then, later things begin to change and you now begin to see some light at the end of the tunnel and a possible way out of the so-called tunnel. A change has happened and there's hope. Others before you may have passed on, but you're still there for whatever the reason. Or, having things go down the drain no matter what, at a particular time when you thought it would never happen. Then again, the unforeseen happens and the picture has changed. The wind is now right and you have clear sailing, and the weather is now perfect for you to sail toward and achieve your goal. I can go on, however, I ask you again, "Do you believe in miracles?" I do because al of the above has happened to yours truly. Miracles do happen! Think about it! Really think about it!

This is H P signing off and wishing you that the bird of plenty give you peace, tranquility, good health and happiness. Until we meet again, I love you to the moon and back. God Bless!

YOU HAVE TO BREAK THINGS TO FIX THINGS

We have choices everyday to wrestle with the current plot in our lives or find the possible joy of putting things back together through a wider experience of life. In spite of problems we all face, each of us is called to nourish ourselves deeply and to see that it is the balance and interplay between body, mind and spirit that contributes to tranquility, good health and happiness.

WELCOME TO MY LITTLE CORNER OF THE WORLD:

Have you ever heard people say, "You have to break things to fix things?" We I have. What people are saying is that in life we ae constantly breaking things in one form or another and they will always need some form of mending etc. For instance, you have a relationship with someone very dear to you and you get into an argument with them and chaos erupts like a volcano. It's like breaking a priceless piece of art. You now try and pick up the pieces etc. You now realize that prior to the explosion, you had a beautiful relationship. But, for whatever reason you did not handle or express yourself the way you thought you did or should of. You assumed that you did.

Remember, my friends that when you assume things you are making an ass out of you and me. It's spelled ASS-U-ME: assume. Think about it! Now we start the mending; to fix things. We are determined, this time, to fix things right. This is what we should have done to begin with. Fortunately, we were able to fix it, and fix it right. We had to break it first in order to fix it right. Think about it! Really think about it!

This is H P signing off and wishing you that the bird of plenty give you peace, tranquility, good health and happiness. I love you to the moon and back! God Bless!

YOU WILL BE SURPRISED AS TO WHAT YOU WILL SEE AND HEAR IF YOU LISTEN

In order to honor our hearts and unfold our true self into the world we must be willing to truly listen to others who have taken the higher path. Laughter and wit are part of the package of wisdom and knowledge, the CARE package we carry into the future. Consciousness Awareness and the Reflective Energy of Laughter can slow down the fearful energy of the daily world.

WELCOME TO MY LITTLE CORNER OF THE WORLD:

Yogi Bera, former catcher for the New York Yankees had many witty, interesting and informative sayings that he shared with his fans and the word in general. One of his many quotes, "It's not over until it's over," was quite a conversation piece for many years. He came up later with a sequel to that quote. He stated or said, "You will be surprised as to what you will see and hear if you listen." Think about that one!

You know, many of us in conversation or whatever have a tendency to wander off into space and really not hear or see what the other person is trying to relate or express to us etc. You have to listen because that's how you learn. And you will see things also in a different perspective as a rule. You have to listen and not be afraid to ask questions. You have to join in and participate in whatever is going on etc. In doing so, and I quote, "You will be surprised as to wat you will see and hear if you listen." Thank you Yogi Bera, wherever you are, for your fantastic witty sayings. It truly gives the so-called intellectual a conversation piece of wit, that they will discuss for a very long time. Think about it! I mean really think about it!

This is H P signing off and wishing you that the bird of plenty give you peace, tranquility, good health and happiness. Until we meet again I love you to the moon and back. God Bless!

BE CAREFUL: STRAIGHT TREES OFTEN HAVE CROOKED ROOTS

We must evaluate life and potential friends by great care so as to see real opportunities and growth with true friendship. After many years we are aware of the preciousness of our bodies, true personalities, family, and happy friends. The bridge between daily life and eternity is the wisdom and joy that is passed on between generations. As the great prophets have taught us in the holy texts, we must be prepared to separate the crooked roots and chapters of our life's experience from the greater Tree of ongoing Life.

WELCOME TO MY LITTLE CORNER OF THE WORLD:

In life we will be facing many situations where appearance can and will be very deceiving. We could be dealing with a situation where people, business transactions, health, the arts etc. are involved. There is a saying, "Be careful because straight trees often have crooked roots." Think about that! I mean really think about that!

You know, there may be a time where you are dealing with persons that may impress you from the very beginning as to honesty, integrity etc. But, as you get more involved with these individuals, it becomes more apparent that you were wrong in your judgement. You judged the book by it's cover.

Then, there are business dealings where you get involved in a deal that you cannot refuse. It's the so-called perfect business transaction. But alas, the deal that you could not refuse, You do refuse! Because, as you do further discovery, there is a scent that makes you back off. And then, there are health situations where maybe the prescription prescribed, was not the right prescription for you. Or, getting involved in the Arts i.e. paintings etc. that turn out to be copies and not the originals. Again, be careful because, "Straight trees often have crooked roots." Think about it! I mean really think about it!

This is H P signing off and wishing you that the bird of plenty give you peace, tranquility, good health and happiness. Until we meet again I love you to the moon and back! God Bless!

A BED TIME STORY FOR THE MIND AND SOUL

We all have had good and bad dreams. One American philosopher who loved Freud once said, "the true ontology of Life is the world of dreams." Indeed, learning to die is learning to live fully. To be a soul in a body, to see, hear, touch, feel life through the heart, this is a continuous wonder. We are, perhaps, spiritual beings living in a material body that will return to the realm of spirit. This was the view of David Bohm, student of Einstein, who became convinced that life goes on to higher Life. H.P. Ames leads the way!

WELCOME TO MY LITTLE CORNER OF THE WORLD:

You're getting ready to retire to bed. You're tired, but not that tired. As a child, your mom and dad would tell you a bed time story, to help you go to sleep. Now that we are older, we still need that bed time story for the mind and soul to help us go to sleep. However, instead of mom and dad telling us the story, we as adults are now telling the story in our mind as we try to go to sleep. It's called reflections. We start to dream of the past, the future, and of the things we would like to see happen.

Then, besides the so-called good dreams, there are the so-called bad dreams that disrupt our peaceful sleep to the point where we have a restless and a bad night. That's life. It is what it is. However, we can in a sense, avoid some of the so-called restless and bad nights by having or dreaming of a "bed time story for the mind as well as the soul." As in the play "The Man from La Mancha," to dream the impossible dream. To dream of the good things that have happened to you. The wonderful memories that no one can take away you. To count your blessings and not sheep, whereby the impossible dream becomes the possible dream!

Yes! A "bed time story for the mind and soul." Sleep well my friends and have a good night!

This is H P signing off and wishing you that the bird of plenty give you peace, tranquility, good health and happiness. Until we meet again, I love you to the moon and back! God Bless!

BE HAPPY IN YOUR WORK

A marvelous tour of the world can take place from your Little Corner of the World. The American author, H.P., has given us much to think about in the adventures of Life! We are being prepared for great compassion, forgiveness, and wisdom of the other side. In our hearts, we understand the uniqueness and value of our lives while we already feel the presence of eternity. Each day is full of so many simple moments of beauty. That is why we must do our work to pass on the importance of taking the higher path. Yes, Life is sacred.

WELCOME TO MY LITTLE CORNER OF THE WORLD:

Every day, as a rule we go to work i.e. to the office, the school where we teach, the hospital where we work and our other places of work etc. Whether it's our work in general, or our profession, it is what it is, day in and day out and for some of us this becomes a chore, a routine and not fun. It's how we perform that will determine the quality of our work.

We should always perform towards perfection and not just okay. It's what we called in the old days, pride of workmanship, profession of what we are capable of doing. And, in doing so, we make our contributions to society and to the world whereby making a better world.

In order to accomplish this, we have to be as stated by Cheseu Hiakawa in the movie, "The Bridge on the River Kwai," "Be happy in your work!" With this attitude and posture your capabilities and contributions become untouchable. Do and choose the type of work and profession that will make you happy, so that you look forward to going to work and being able to contribute and do your part in making this a better planet in choosing your so-called "Be happy in your Work" profession. Remember, as I mentioned in one of my previous broadcasts, never use money to determine wealth and happiness, ergo, never determine wealth and happiness by money. Do things because you are and will be happy in doing them. Again, "Be happy in your work," and you will see the difference that it will make in your life. Think about it! Really think about it! This is H P signing off and wishing you that the bird of plenty give you peace, tranquility, good health and happiness. Until we meet again I love you to the moon and back! God Bless!

PAY FORWARD

In this time of big changes and big challenges, "Pay Forward" is another way of applying the Golden Rule of Life to all situations. Whenever we set in motion any form of mental or physical good activity we also set in motion the conditions for good reciprocal responses. Unconditional service to humanity and forward thinking is the Golden Rule that encourages others to follow, and opens the door for a positive future.

-J.J. Hurtak, Ph.D. Author of *The Keys of Enoch®*

Welcome to my little corner of the world:

Many of us I'm sure have heard people say, "It's Payback Time!" But how many of us have heard people say, "It's Pay Forward Time?", probably not many. What do we mean or think of when we say, "It's Pay Forward Time"?

Well, by paying forward, we try to do things before they actually happen...helping a neighbor, a friend, a stranger, doing something nice, not only for our fellow man, but for our planet also.

Being considerate, understanding, helpful etc. In doing so these things become contagious and people will reciprocate by doing likewise. Positives beget positives, and negatives beget negatives. Be positive, Pay Forward!

An example, I was driving on the freeway and up ahead was a stranded car and persons. As I drove closer to the distressed party, a car passed me by and drove ahead and then stopped along side the of the freeway. The person in the car then backed up to the distressed party and offered help, to the joy of the persons in trouble.

I then stopped up ahead and also backed up and asked if there was anything that I could do to help. I was told that everything was under control. I then continued on.

Several weeks later I was in an area called The Spanish Landing. This was in the San Diego area. I was parked and a car pulled up and a person got out of the car and said that he and his wife were from out of town and visiting the San Diego area.

They were lost and were looking for a medium priced hotel to stay at while in San Diego, something close to everything of interest Etc.

I gave them directions to something really nice, perfect location to everything; Balboa Park, The Gas Lamp District Etc.

I then realized that they were totally confused again. I then told them that I would be more than happy to take them there if they would follow me in the car. They proceeded to follow me to their destination. When we arrived they were totally pleased and happy and could not believe that someone would go out of their way to drive and make sure they would not get lost again.

They were overwhelmed by a stranger helping a stranger. They asked if they could re-pay me in any way. I said it was my pleasure and the next time they see someone in need, help them, Pay Forward, do unto others as you would want others to do unto you. The Golden Rule! Pay Forward!

In doing so you see and feel the joy of helping your fellow man. It will be priceless! Think about it, I mean really think about it!

This is HP signing off and wishing you that the bird of plenty give you good health, peace, tranquility and happiness. Until we meet again, I love you to the moon and back. God Bless!

LOVING;
THE SECOND TIME AROUND

True love overcomes the voids of life. True love is true life in the ability to transform and transcend the little vacuums of life and passions in life that pass so one can grow with love on all levels of life. True love is the experience of greater wisdom.

-J.J. Hurtak, Ph.D. Author of *The Keys of Enoch®*

Welcome to My Little Corner of the World

Good evening Alan and welcome to my little corner of the world.

The word "Love" is a very powerful, healing, soothing and remedial word. It's a word not often, but should be used, frequently. Have you ever loved someone or something so much that it hurts? At the time you embrace those moments with all your strength and love. You capture the moment and never want to let go.

Time passes on and later, those moments are gone, no longer there. You are now lost in an empty time zone. This goes on for a period of time Etc. You now feel lost and in limbo and feel that there is nothing more to look forward to. Not So! How wrong can you be!

Remember, Patience is a virtue. As time goes by you come across moments that open new avenues of life. New opportunities, maybe far superior than the previous ones. A new love, whereby love becomes more beautiful than imagined.

Now the new love may not replace the original wonderful moments of the past, but they can help in replacing the so-called void that you were experiencing prior to your new love. Then again, the new love could be the true love that you did not have in the past.

Remember, Love can be wonderful and beautiful the second time around. Friends, remember that we can incorporate Love in our daily life whereby making our lives on this planet a lot happier, healthier and above all more peaceful, tranquil and less hate.

Let's have Love not War! Think about it, I mean really think about it. This is HP signing off and wishing you that the bird of plenty give you health, peace, tranquility and happiness. Until we meet again, I love you to the moon and back. God Bless!

EVERYONE HAS SOMETHING IN THEIR PAST THAT THEY WOULD LIKE TO FORGET

> Positives beget positives and negatives beget negatives. One should end the endless cycle of getting trapped in negative scenarios. Allow negative memories to pass by, and get on with the work of transforming life through positive thinking.
>
> –J.J. Hurtak, Ph.D. Author of *The Keys of Enoch®*

Welcome to My Little Corner of the World

Alan, everyone has something in their past that they would like to forget. We are human, and as a result we have done things in the past that now as we think about it, we would like to forget those things. Things that we have done or said or thought of doing.

For instance, we might have done things that were dumb, stupid, ridiculous, crazy etc. at that particular time. By the same token we might also have said or thought of things that may have been just as ridiculous as the things done in the past.

Now in doing so, its not a matter of trying to forget the past. It should be a matter of benefitting by the things were experienced at the time, so that we do not do it again.

Now, by taking this posture we are not dwelling on the past because dwelling on the past can prevent your future. So, you benefit by the past and move on to bigger and better things in life. You are not trying to erase the past in this particular case, you're benefitting by the so-called past and moving on.

Remember, positives beget positives and negatives beget negatives. Let's think positive! You can do it! Think about it, really think about it!

This is HP signing off and wishing you that the bird of plenty give you Health, Peace, Tranquility and Happiness. Until we meet again, I love you to the moon and back. God Bless!

BEING AT THE RIGHT PLACE AT THE RIGHT TIME

Being at the right place at the right time is a subtle lesson of life, Your real presence and your real self does not come from some imagined future or some imaged past, but using the power of the timelessness of service to humanity by taking the higher road

-J.J. Hurtak, Ph.D. Author of *The Keys of Enoch®*

Welcome to my Little Corner of the World

How many of us have experienced being at the right place at the right time? Some of us, but we did not know it at the time. Being at the right place... Like one summer I was at the beach in San Diego, CA. And one sunny day I decided to bask in the sun on the bayside of South Mission Beach.

As I approached the bay I heard a mom screaming for help. Her very young son was way out in the middle of the bay in an inner tube raft by himself. Somehow, at first being very close to the shoreline, the tide and the current of the bay seemed to have quickly drifted the boy further out into the bay. Being a week day, there was no one around at the time to help.

The boy was approximately $\frac{3}{4}$ to 1 mile from the shore. The boy's mother was frantic as you would expect. Hearing the screams, and seeing the boy's mother along the shoreline etc.

I dashed into the water and started to swim as fast as possible. I swam, and finally reached the boy who was snug in the inner tube. He was frightened and extremely happy to see me. I was able to get the boy and myself safely to shore. When we got to the shore the mother was ecstatic and very grateful that I was able to help to get her son back to shore safe and sound.

You know, it was a great and wonderful feeling to be able to help someone in need. Doing unto others as you would have others doing unto you. Helping and loving thy neighbor and being at the right place at the right time.

Hey, this is HP signing off and wishing you that the bird of plenty give you Peace, Tranquility and Good Health. Until we meet again, I love you to the moon and back. God Bless!

YOU CAN'T ALWAYS HAVE OR GET WHAT YOU WANT - BUT YOU CAN TRY

The greater our dreams, the greater the effort we must muster on the roadway of opportunity.

Real education is not in book-learning, but in letting go of subjective and objective frustrations and painful doubts so that our mind can adjust itself to using the highest potential to know that there are *no problems, only solutions.*

-J.J. Hurtak, Ph.D. Author of *The Keys of Enoch®*

Welcome to my Little Corner of the World:

In life we have our moments where we would like to have certain things happen to us. We may not be able to achieve those goals, but we can certainly try.

There is a saying that if you're going to dream, Dream Big! To dream or try to do the so-called impossible, may not be so impossible if we really try and try hard. In doing so we just may surprise ourselves to no end.

Abe Lincoln did not have a formal education and had many setbacks and failures in his life. His dream was to be able to make a contribution to his fellow man and society, and to be able to do something for his beloved country.

A Big Dream for someone that did not have a formal education, and a person who had many setbacks and failures.

This did not stop Abe Lincoln from trying and doing things to the best of his ability. As time went on, he decided to run for the office of the president of the country he dearly loved. He became President and during his tenure as president he delivered a speech in 1863 called The Gettysburg Address. Upon completion of the speech there was a silence for several minutes and then a thunderous ovation from the audience. They were hypnotized by his speech. Little did he realize how well he could speak. He was president of his beloved country despite his tremendous adversities.

Remember, you can't always have what you want, but you can try, and Abe Lincoln tried and did get what he wanted. Again, all you have to do is just try and you may surprise yourself and others. Think about it. I mean really think about it!

This is HP signing off and wishing you that the bird of plenty bring you Peace, Tranquility, and good health. Until we meet again, I love you to the moon and back. God Bless!

BEFORE YOU WONDER, AM I DOING THINGS RIGHT ASK AM I DOING THE RIGHT THINGS

There are three basic questions we must all face in this life. They are simple but their consequences are profound. Honesty with ourselves opens a true pathway. Dishonesty closes the door in the long run. In these three questions *live all one needs to know* in the practical world, that is, assuming one desires to be wholesome, loving, and true to the rest of one's mission in Life.

-J.J. Hurtak, Ph.D. Author of *The Keys of Enoch®*

Welcome to my Little Corner of the World:

Many times we do things and many times they don't turn out the way we planned. At the time, they seamed to be the right thing to do. The problem is that we do not take the time to really think things out and analyze the pros and cons of the situation.

The so-called "what if" theory. What if it does not work out? And if it does, is it worth the price we have to pay? In a previous podcast I had mentioned that someone once said, and I quote, "The world is yours for the taking, but there are three questions we should ask ourselves first:

Question #1. Do I want it? Question #2. What's it going to cost me? And Question #3. Is it worth it?

Question #3 is the one we should give much thought to because this is the price we are going to have to pay. What you decide can and probably could determine your future. So I say to you, ask yourself, am I doing things right? Am I doing the right things? Think about it.

This is HP signing off and wishing you that the bird of plenty give you Peace, Tranquility, and Good Health. Until we meet again I love you to the moon and back. God Bless!